Company I 366th Infantry

by

Harold E. Russell, Jr.

RoseDog❧Books

PITTSBURGH, PENNSYLVANIA 15222

For more information or to order additional books, please contact:
RoseDog Books
701 Smithfield Street
Third Floor
Pittsburgh, Pennsylvania 15222
U.S.A.
1-800-834-1803
www.rosedogbookstore.com

TABLE OF CONTENTS

INTRODUCTION

In writing my experience as a member and a part of the 366th Infantry Regt., may not be as technical or documentary as some one who was in Headquarter. However you may understand some of the prejudices that were felt as far down as the Company level and line soldier.

Being a member of an all Black Infantry Regt. a one of a kind, is a proud distinction. I feel many people are not aware of the many good and outstanding accomplishments that derive from this all Black Infantry Regt.

Much of the following pages are things I've personally been involved in. While other items were stories that were heard, which helped make a more closely attached group of men, from all walks of life. I entered the service as a volunteer at 17 years of age, because quite a few of my friends had gone into the service, either from selective services or the Federal activation of the 369th Regt.

I am writing this book from the view of a "foot soldier," assigned to company I, 366th Inf. Regt., I may never have this published, but I have enjoyed reviewing some of the events. While some other made me wonder how we were able to survive the treatment we received as a black American Soldier.

My wife and sister kept telling me to write my experiences, but not having the background for writing I kept putting it off. A neighbor, Rev. Hooper, during a conversation said he was writing a book, and I replied I was also. Then he said let's see where we are on October 1995 which would be a year later. Then and there I applied myself to putting what I could remember on paper.

History of the 366th Infantry Regiment

The 366th Infantry was organized at camp Dodge, Iowa, in November 1917. The regiment served overseas during World War I as part of the 92 Division, National Army, and earned credit for battle participation as follows:

St. Die Sector (Lorraine) August 23 - Sept 20 1918: Meuse-Argonne Sector Sept. 26 - Oct 5 1918. Marbach Sector (Lorraine) October 8 - Nov 1918.

It is entitled to Lorraine and Meuse-Argonna Battle Streamers for Colors. The regiment returned to the United States and was demobilized at Fort Oglethrope, Georgia, March 25, 1919. One July 26, 1941, it was reconstituted and consolidated with the 366 Infantry which was organized December 16, 1940 and made active February 10, 1941.

(A Quote from the Pictorial History of the 366th Infantry Ft. Deven, Mass. 1941)

Chapter I

Induction April 1941

It all started when I was seventeen years old in 1941, when the 369th New York National Guard was federalized and was sent to camp Drum then to camp Edwards, Mass.

Never realizing how many of the fellows I knew were in the National Guard. Most of them a year or two older than I was. My cousin C. Martin McNeal, who lived on 136th Street. We would go to St Nicholas Park and on the way we picked up several of the boys and play in the Park. Then there was a group I played with in the Dunbar 150th between 7th and 8th Avenue plus another group in the Harlem River Houses all seemed to disappear. Well I got the feeling of being left out not old enough for the draft, but wanted to catch up with the 369th. I decided to volunteer.

My father was working for the Penn Rail Road and came in to New York rarely. So I turned to my "Uncle" Sam Faide, my godmother's husband who was on the draft board where there was an office in the Dunbar Apartment Complex. He signed for me, which allowed me to volunteer for the draft. Shortly, I was called down to the White Hall Street for my physical. Seems that something was wrong with my heart and they sent me to a specialist on West End Drive in the area of 90's avenue. Since I was staying with my Aunt I didn't like to ask her for money knowing it was scarce. I walked from 149 street and 8th Avenue to the Doctor's office, West End Drive and 90 Street. Whatever it was that the Doctor's in White Hall heard, didn't seem to be there when the specialist checked. I was told to report back to White Hall for induction.

April 25, 1941, a large group of draftees and volunteers left the induction center for Penn Station, then by train to Fort Dix, NJ.

Chapter II

Beginning of Military Service

Arrive at Ft Dix's. I was then separated with all the other Blacks (Negro then) and sent to an all black unit. That was the beginning of the separation of Color. We were marched to our "Company" Area. What happen from then on is cloudy. Some of the things that I do remember was we had to get haircuts, issued clothing, which Hackney and myself were six footers and were long legged and slim couldn't get a pair of pants to fit us or shoes size 12C, for a week or more. Bedding, equipment such as Knapsack, eating utensils, leggings, we didn't get rifles till later.

Then we met Sergeant Branch. I will never forget this man. He was our Drill Sergeant. He made himself known to us by saying, "You've heard of Drill Sergeants, well that's who I am." He was not only a drill sergeant, but a terrible Drill Sergeant. There were also other Non-Commissions Officers and Commissioned Officers, but for the life of me it is Sergeant Branch who was drilled into my memory.

For the next six weeks we drilled, exercised, cleaned the area, and kitchen police (KP). The sergeant asked one day, while we were in formation anyone with previous military training or boy scouting experience should step forward. I was indeed proud of my scouting experience and stepped forward. What that moment of being proud got me was being assigned to the garbage detail. I was hoping for better things. (I learn never to volunteer in the army).

We were issued rifles and while many of us dropped them we quickly learned not to drop them again. For we had to run a couple trips around the parade ground, which was no small area, caring an eight pound heavy rifle over our head, which was no small task. This was done to teach us to hold on to our rifle.

Finally after our six weeks of basic training we were given a weekend pass. Most of us went home to the Big Apple (New York City). That was a real quick weekend. I remember now my Aunt and Uncle got a big kick out of my boot size which was size 12. And while I went to visit my girlfriend, I returned home to find my boots sitting in the middle of the living room floor for everyone to see. I really took all of ribbing that day.

Shortly after our six weeks of boot camp we were shipped to Fort Deven, Mass. From the train depot into the town of Ayers on route to Fort Devens. There we were lined up and assigned to companies. Captain Pierce was our Commanding Officer, Lt Gould Executive Officer, 3 Platoons Lt. Fearing and Ford. Later came Lt. Goode out of Ft. Benny OCS. At first, it was close order drill in the company area. Then the squad separated to drill, later the platoon functioned as a unit with rifle range training. Then came the never ending field maneuvers, hikes or should I say long marches.

The Company that I was assigned to was Company I third platoon. Sgt Whittakers was the Platoon Sgt. Organizing his platoon, the tallest on the right and shortest on the left. I was the tallest and assigned to the 1st squad, Hackney the second and Mahaley the third.

After marking our equipment we were to start our close order drill. When we started receiving instructions from the Cadre we learned that they were not too far ahead of us in combat training. After listening to some of the sergeants who were giving the instructions, I decided if we read the manual, we would and could be better then some of the sgts. We found out that most of the Cadre were privates in Ft. Benning and were sent up to form the Cadre of the 366. One sgt. was giving us instructions on handling the grenades. Now standing in front of the two platoons, Sgt. Johnson took up the grenade and proceeded to call it a canary. Well Lt. Fearing corrected the situation but Mahaley, Whittake and I started a little reading and learning session in Sgt Whittakers room. Mahaley and I were pushing for promotions, since we saw that the Cadre was not much more advanced. Mahaley became proficient in the weapons. I engaged in map reading and communications. I, however, got the short end, since communication Sgt. was only a corporal, and Mahaley went to Buck Sgt. Later I was assigned to a company guide and got my three stripes.

Time passed and we were sent to NCO school. Mahaley and I started a competition between us to out do each other on map reading problems. Mahalely was good with the machine guns and heavy weapons. I went for communication, radio and map reading.

At the end of NCO school there were classes for Karate. I happened to catch hold of one of the Non-Commissioned Officers a hand grip and flipped him over my shoulder [all pure luck]. But after that the fellows wouldn't fool around with me thinking I had all the grips down pat.

Once Captain Pierce asked me to get his car which was up by the Officer's quarters in the parking lot. Now, I never took a driving lesson nor did I have a driver's license. But I thought I knew how to drive, of course. The Capt. had a Ford coupe. I walked over and drove it back with no trouble, I thought. After getting out of the car, I began to smell rubber. Trying to think what could be wrong, I discovered I had drove a couple of miles with the emergency brake on. Needless to say, I didn't tell the captain.

Twenty one dollars a month did not go far. On pay day you had to pay for laundry, $1.50, $2.00 for a coupon book for the PX which left you a grand total of $17.00. Well, car fare to NYC was $5.50 that left $12.00. Bus and train fares to home left you just about broke. This did not include what you may owe around the barracks. Many of the fellows made one trip home then if you were lucky to have someone send money from home you could visit around in Boston or Ayers.

Some 90 day wonders (Officers who took the 90 day OCS training at Ft. Benning) were assigned to the Regt. Lt William Goode was one of them and was assigned to Company I. He was fresh from Ft Benning, without any field clothes. One day he came on the field with his leggings on backward, he looked lost and out of place. I took a liking to him and corrected his leggings. While mentioning to him that he might get a few needed items from the supply, Sgt. Lt. Goode was assigned to the 3rd Platoon and Lt Fearing became the Ex. Officer.

I remember reveille, getting up for roll call. Most times we would have roll call then return to the barracks to clean up and get ready for breakfast. One occasion the 1st Sgt had a "bug up his ass," would run us up to the parade grounds for exercise. One morning I just put on my overcoat and came out for roll call. That happened to be the day he had a "bug." On the parade ground we were told to take off all outer garment for exercise. It got damn cold out there with no clothes on.

Capt. Pierce was the C.O. Ex Off. Lt. Gould, than there was Lt. Ashley, Ford and Fearing. Lt Gould left and Fearing became EX Off.

With the weather so hot field training became almost unbearable but our training continued while other outfits (white) were given training or lectures under trees or other shady places. But our Col. Chase, our operation officer was so intent to make us 1st Class soldiers (or kill us trying) keep the officers on their toes and following the training schedule.

One day during our field training we would see the 101 Calvary training with horses. The temperature reached 90 degrees and some of the horses keeled over. Whether they died or not we didn't find out. But a couple of days after during the Summer, the beef stew we had for dinner was so tough that we started saying that it must be the horses that dropped and now being served as beef.

Around November 1941 some of soldiers who were over age (35) were released and sent home. Then came December 7, 1941 those who didn't get out were held. Those who were discharged started coming back after Christmas.

During this organizing period and Basic Training with the Company, I will probably put a lot out of context, since some of us like myself was away from home for the first time (other then summer camp).

It was a little confusing to have men yelling, cussing, etc., calling you every thing but the son of God. It was hard at first waking up at 5 A.M. making up your bed, washing up, cleaning up the barrack before reveille. Later on we were able to do it much faster, then we started sleeping later.

My first command of Guard duty after making corporal, is something I can laugh at now, but then—

The Sgt. of the guard had taken the guard detail to the Guard House to relieve those on duty. Arriving we went through the guard ceremony. I had the first duty, trying to look the part I was getting ready to post the guard. Calling my guard detail to attention my voice went from bass to soprano. I could feel the blood rushing to my face. Clearing my throat I tried it again, hoping I could regain the command of the Guard who were standing at attention trying not to laugh.

Word came down that those enlisted men who wanted to be promoted would have to attend study classes that were being established by Headquarters.

Capt. Fowler, a graduate from West Point, was the instructor of the NCO Classes. Being a recent graduate from West Point, I think he was trying to put us through the paces as they did in West Point.

When he took us out on the drill field he ran us through the cadence. As they did in the point, every thing was at a quick march. In the classroom every thing was very technical, heavy weapons, guns, map reading. I took the map reading.

When our 1st Sgt. was off on the deep end, I was substituting for him, making out the reports calling the company to formation. I was the

Communication NCO, and spent a lot of time in the office acting as the "duty Sgt." doing office work, helping out in the supply room and other office related duties.

During this time Whittaker and Mahaley took the company on the field, and I held down the company area, doing the morning report going to the 1st Sgt. meeting at HQ. One day Lt. Goode was in the orderly room when the 1st Sgt. was in one of his "good moods." Lt. Goode asked the 1st Sgt., can you whistle? Then he left the office. The Sgt., puzzled, asked me what Lt. Goode meant. I told him that I thought it meant that when you're a Pvt. doing a lot of guard duty the Pvt's do a lot of whistling while out on guard duty by themselves.

Interesting looking back, some of the men, some much older than I, would not take any type of leadership. All waiting for the one year conscription to end and be released from military duty. Some were college graduates, some had good jobs before they came in. Listening to them was interesting. One fellow was in the CCC Camp for several years. William Martin (Bill) he seemed to know a little about all kinds of camp life. Or listening to the Cadre with there life in Ft. Benning. Then there was the street smart of Harlem, the slickers.

During the summer of 41, I remember one of our many dress parades. Col Chase and Col Hamilton stated that when they are in Boston and see soldiers walking about in Boston, they wanted to be able to say those properly dressed soldiers were from the 366th Inf. Reg. That seemed to be the clue for all 1st Sgt's who give out the weekend passes, that if they weren't properly dressed (with Pro Kit) they were denied the pass. Those caught in town improperly dressed and were reported to the Capt. or 1st Sgt., were restricted for a period of time.

I've heard that Col. Queen and Hamilton remarked proudly of the way the 366 carried themselves in town. Even when they were in NY (Big Apple) looking out the window on 7th Ave., they would say they can tell the "6's" from the other soldiers. Most of the men would bitch of the hard discipline but we all proudly claim our rights of being in the "All Black Infantry," commanded by all Black Officers.

The famous silk stocking NY National Guard 69th was up in Devens training prior to going over seas. When they got their orders they let it be known that they were selling a lot of their clothes and equipment that they couldn't take over seas. (Mostly tailored made items) Well the 6's were known to dress well, and bought a lot of special made things, campaign hats, short winter coats, etc. There were a lot of well dressed 6's after the 69 left Devens.

One day we were told that there were a lot of surplus clothes up at HQ Supply (X marked clothing) that we could get at no charge. These clothes were army issued originally but had been damaged and altered for one reason or another. I went and picked out a short overcoat, a regular army coat that was cut down to finger tip length. These clothes were so marked with a big X inside them so we couldn't turn them in for new issue. Well I started wearing my short coat around after formation and was stopped many times and questioned why I damaged regular issue clothing. After awhile the officers got used to the X clothing and let up on the questioning.

Rambling—

It seems that we are ignored, suppressed, etc., until our skills or muscles are needed. One fall season we were asked to pick apples in upstate New York. We had our own separate facilities, we were a good distance from the others on the post.... When they needed a life guard in there section of the lake, we were called on. The officers at HQ volunteer our services. We had our own life guards.

A request was sent to all companies asking for lifeguards for Mirror Lake in the late Spring of 1942. Mirror Lake was at the bottom of the hill in the rear of M Company. It was a running lake about a mile long and 1/2 mile wide. Some places such as were the other inhabitants of the post used (White) was a little wider.

I applied and took the test. Lt. Martin gave the test. Several of the fellows in our company applied as well as the rest of the Regt. I passed the test and was accepted with several others. Being the ranking NCO I was put in charge not that I was the best swimmer. Being in charge meant the maintenance, cleaning, instructions and the planning of large activities. Once the Lake was officially open, off duty personnel would swim during the day and the troops after duty would come down to cool off before sundown. Weekends were the busies time. One Saturday afternoon several of the "good" swimmers were enjoying the water by the float, which I happened to be there. One of the fellows who was in the water maybe a foot or two from the float got cramps and started to drown. I tried to reach him from the float and he was just a little too far to grab. Then I jumped in between him and the float, thinking to grab him and pass him to the fellows on the float when up came his knee into my groin and his arm around my neck. My first thought was we both are going to drown. After struggling for a while, I realized that we both were in trouble and started taking him down deeper when he released me. I was than able to apply life saving techniques which I should have done at first. I brought him in and boy did I get a razing from the fellows on the float.

Another big day was when Col. Hamilton called me to HQ to inform me that I was to start preparing to give swimming lessons to the Regt. There was six lifeguards for this big task. In the true 366 tradition we accomplished the task given us.

In 1943 the WAACS and Nurses were training at Devens. The nurses and the WAACS were using one end of the lake. One morning I was again called to HQ and given a very hard but delightful task. I was directed to go over to the Nurses and WAC area to help them with the swimming lessons. This enjoyable duty didn't last too long, but I enjoyed the little time I was assigned to assist them. One weekend which started off bad was when several of the lifeguards arrived to clean up and prepare for the day; put the boats out in the water, check the float to see it was secured and other cleanup maintenance. While we were in the shed changing clothes when one of the "good" swimmers who had finished changing and standing around waiting for us, decided he'd run down and be the first one in. When we came out of the shed and looked for him he was halfway across the lake. This was against all safety rules, to swim across the lake by ones self. We yelled for him to return, but he evidently didn't hear us, or just wanted to keep going. Just about 3/4 of the way across he began to flounder. I told the others to grab the boat and get out there. I went and jumped in and raced out their. When I got to the point where he went down, I started looking for him. By this time the others were there diving too. I was tired and swam to the shore to catch my breath and try to judge the current, but all of our efforts were to no avail. About a week later after dragging the bottom he floated up near the end of the lake. Orders were issued that no one enters the lake without the lifeguard on duty on station and no one was to swim beyond the ropes without using the buddy system or a boat alongside.

The Spring of 44, the Regt. planned a "March," and amphibious operation. The troops were in full field pack and all company vehicles. At one end of the lake where it was a stream feeding the lake, was the route of the march. The water was one to two feet deep. The whole Regt. passed through, there were lots of mishaps but all in all a good exercise.

Summer of '42 Women Auxiliary Corps (WAC) came to Ft. Devens. They were assigned to an area not far from our area. A good walking distance, naturally I made myself known. Later I was ordered to go to the area to put in a public address system from the orderly room to the three barracks. One day while working in one of the barracks putting wire up, it was about 10 A.M. There were several WAC's either sleeping (had night duty) and others just milling around. To my surprise a command of attention was called while I was up on a pole stringing wire. I came down and came to attention best I could with wire and tools in hand. Well the General took one look at me and came directly to me and asked what business I had in a women's barracks. I recognized the General, Gen. B.O. Davis. He sputtered a second after I explained my duties. He told the WAC Capt. who was with him to make sure that the orderly was with him each time he goes into a barrack were the women were. With that I was ordered to carry on.

After the WAC's arrived it changed a lot of activities on post. More lectures of wine, women and sex. This brings to mind when one of our chaplains was talking to us about women and sex àt a gathering, don't remember if it was a Battalion or Regt. activity. But after telling about a little story of a cat crossing the railroad tracks, when a train came and ran over its tail. Turning to see what happened to his tail one of the wheels ran over his head. Then he said the moral of this story is don't lose your head over a little piece of tail. Several days later the same chaplain was caught in a car behind the officer club with a WAC. Needless to say he was transferred. I remember once I was sent to the WAC area for something during the late afternoon when most of the WAC's were in the area in their barracks. Walking through their company area with all the girls looking, I received the treatment that I thought was normally given to women walking among men. The WAC's were whistling and keeping time with my walking. It was an experience, and the orderly room seemed to get longer and further away.

Chapter III

After December 7th

After completing basic drills and company maneuvers we advanced to Battalion maneuvers, then Regt'l. Then repeat it all again until December 7, 1941. . . .

Then came guard duty various railroad crossing bridges and strategic points in New England. With the scare of sabotage the Regt. was sent all over New England. A detachment from Co. I was sent to Socko-Bidderford, Maine to guard the railroad bridges in this area. Lt. Green was in charge of this detail. Lt. Green was from Boston, which may account for his orders about breakfast. Since we were on twenty-four hours duty, some of the men would come off duty at 8 A.M. So Lt. Green decided that a breakfast meal was too light for men coming off duty at 8 A.M. and ordered the restaurant to serve franks and beans. We had meal arrangement with a local restaurant which we had meal tickets. Our complaints to Lt. Green were to no avail. After settling down and a duty rooster made up etc., where we were lodged, which was a caboose on a railroad siding. While the fellows were off duty we would visit the bars, not much else to do in the town of Sock. One bar we went into where we were received like hero's. After a period of time drinking, we got ready to leave and asked for our bill. The bartender pointed to a large glass (5 gal) jar filled with money saying that all military personnel were to drink free. The money was taken out of it. That was money the bar patrons contributed. We stated that we are stationed here and would deplete the funds which was all to no avail. About a month later when we were relieved to return to Ft. Devens, we took up a collection and replenished some of the money we drank up. At another bar in Bidderford we were sitting at tables drinking having a light bull session. One of the town's bullies decided he didn't like the "colored" in the bar. He started a fight with some men and the shortest there was George Walcott who got hit with a beer bottle. George left the bar in a hurry, about 15 minutes later George had returned with his M-1 rifle and was ready to kill the SOB. I had to talk fast while several of us subdued him. The police and our men were able to quiet things down. An article in the local papers the next day stated something like the town drunks started a fight with some of the armed forces in town and was locked up for disorderly conduct. Shortly after that we were relieved and returned to Ft. Devens.

Montpellier, Vermont, winter of 1942. Company I on the road again, this time a detachment of about thirty men were sent to Montpellier, Vermont to guard the railroad bridges in the area. We were stationed in a house on the edge of town. It was cold but dry, it snowed about every three days or so. Up there nobody attempted to clean the snow from the sidewalks etc. The streets were kept clear and snow was piled high on the side of the road. We were told not to be fooled by the temperature, to dress warm. The dry weather could fool you by not feeling the cold until you were almost frozen. Other than the guard duty and trying to survive in the cold weather, nothing of interest in this place in the winter. Several times our vehicles would slip over in the snow and had to be pulled out. I don't remember any incidents that may or may not have happened there. If it were anything big, I believe I would have remembered. Except the time we were short of rations due to the snow. Several of us went out and killed a deer. Not having a real cook, I cut up the deer and made a large pot of stew. I guess everybody was hungry since no complaints. It was a short duty I don't believe we stayed more than a month there.

Another assignment was Westover Field, Mass., in the spring of 1943. Part of the company was sent to Westoverfield Airport to guard the airplanes on the base. Lt. Wm. Goode was in charge. Off duty "guards" were free to go to town. Springfield was close by. Lots of military contracts there so there were lots of women in the factory. Even though they were working they still were looking for a good time and the expense of us poor soldiers. I believe the incident that brought our assignment to a short stay was after one weekend when first assigned to Westoverfield. I took in a movie or thought I was. I went to the theater and paid for my ticket, went in and took a seat to my liking. Just as I was getting comfortable, the usher came to me and told me I was sitting in the wrong section. I asked how come?

He told me I had to sit with my outfit down front. I asked what outfit and where were they sitting? He told me some service organization down toward the front of the theater. I told him that was not my outfit and since I was not assigned to any particular area I'd sit right here. He asked me to come to the back so as to straighten things out. I left my seat and went back with him. I asked him for his name and serial number when an officer appeared. The usher explained the situation with my injection. I must have become loud for the officer asked me to leave the theater. After a few words, plus asking for my money back, he went to the ticket offices and gave me my admission price back. I made a beeline back to the "company" area, and pulled some paper and began typing a letter to the post command, Corp. Commander, Regt'l Commander, and our company commander. About this time Lt. Goode came in to see what I was doing that late in the Office. I told him and he read the letter, told me I could send it, and started helping me compose the letter, which we did and mailed out that night.

About a week or so later we were recalled. We rejoined our company. I don't remember if I personally received a reply, but I remember something was said to the caption which indicated the colonel had said something to him. The regiment was not sent back to Westoverfield, Mass.

Since we received such unmilitary treatment on the base, most of our free time was in Springfield or Boston. Activities were limited to black areas. Not only was it my first time in the town, but my first time aware of a heavy fog.

Coming back one night, after missing the company truck, I had to take a cab. It was a little hazy in town but when we got in open country the fog was so thick that the headlights bounced back at you. You could hardly see the hood of the cab. The driver said he could make it. He started driving on the left side of the road with the door open looking down at the solid white line, while I was having a heart attack worrying about another car coming head on. If I was "under the weather" leaving town I was real sober when we arrived at camp. That was the longest ten miles that I could remember.

Chapter IV

Camp A.P. Hill, VA

In the spring of 1944 we were told we were going to AP Hill Va. to receive training for combat for six weeks than to be shipped over seas. We arrived in AP Hill and were put up in a "tent city." We were setup and started training. Weekend passes were available. Some went to NYC some to Washington, Philadelphia. I remember the first weekend leaving AP Hill and catching the train, roughly 500 or more were catching the first train out to Washington and point north. When the train pulled in and all of us military soldiers of the Army of United States got on and attempted to find seats were we could. When the conductor came through the train stating the train wouldn't move until all of us colored people got in the colored car. Well for one thing there were too many of us to get into the colored car. Two, we were not accustomed to a segregated travel. Three, we were in uniform. The conductor was saying the train would not move until we all got into one car. Nobody moved or even attempted to go to the colored car. The train stayed there for about one half hour. The conductor went into the station ticket office and probably was told to move on since another train was on schedule.

In he meantime, after I (we) got back from our weekend, we were told what went on in town. It seems like a few of the stores and restaurants wouldn't sell to the soldiers, except through the back door, etc. Well, the way I heard it, was that the 366 Inf. did a little damage to the town. Bars, bowling alleys, restaurants were a little rearranged.

Well our six weeks of training in AP Hill was cut short. A week or so later, more trucks than I've seen in one area were there to take us to Ind. It seems that the town petition to have us moved out of the area. Well we left tent city by truck through West Virginia, Ohio to Camp Atterbury, Ind.

At Camp Atterbury we had barracks, and proceeded to do our six weeks of intensive training. Besides our training, I remember the hot arid fields, bugs, rabbits and lots of flat land.

We ran into some WAC's that were in Ft. Devens. It seems that they left Devens then to New Mexico then reassigned to Camp Atterbury. At the service club it appeared to be a big reunion of the WAC's and those of the 366th Inf.

Arriving by truck from AP Hill, VA we were assigned to our area. Our arrival in Atterbury was the home base of the Buffalo 92nd Div. All the facilities were open to us since the 92 was a black Div. There were ample clubs and PX's to go to. When in Devens the post facilities were all white. Here I had my glasses fixed and dental work done by black medical personnel.

After settling down we were free to go to the post exchange and service club. We were in an area with our own facilities. I don't remember seeing any other units, since we had medical units etc. manned by blacks, I found out since I needed my glasses repaired.

Drilling was usual. Booties scheduled a lot of field work and firing range. The weather was hot and plenty of rabbits. Few of the fellows were trying to catch some, said they were good eating.

We stayed in Atterbury for about six weeks. I was able to get to Chicago. I had an Aunt there who had help raise me. Visiting her, I was totally surprised at seeing her, for she had gained extremely lots of weight. I didn't recognize her at first. It was a short weekend, but I am glad of the visit. I also visited Indianapolis on a weekend. Met some people who were from New York living there.

The first night I went to the service club, after learning that the WAC's were there, I wanted to see who was there I knew from Devens. Well it didn't take long since the WAC's knew we were there. So they were looking, I guess as hard as we were. I knew some from Devens, so it was like old home week. One girl who took a liking to me, told me her parents were coming up and wanted to meet me. Well I didn't know what she had in mind, so I got assigned to charge of quarters for the weekend. Never did meet the parents. The six weeks went fast, for we had finished our six weeks of combat training and were being shipped to Newport News, VA by train. The train ride was uneventful. All the shades were pulled down so we couldn't look out and people couldn't see in to say there was a troop movement.

Chapter V

Hampton Roads, VA

We pulled into Hampton Roads, our port of debarkation. We boarded a Liberty Ship, for many of us it was the first time on a large vessel. Single file we went up the gang plank calling out our name, and assigned to a section and bunk. We received our meal tag, color coded so as to feed section at a time.

Arriving at Newport News, VA we were not allowed to make any calls home or elsewhere. No sense in writing because the officers would have to censor the letters and that meant probably it wouldn't get mailed until we arrived at our destination. After being assigned to our compartment, we were told what time to line up for chow and other facts of the ship. The word went out for ship details. As usual most soldiers won't volunteer for anything. But I thought about just two meals a day and the crew got three meals. So I just volunteered for the galley.

We were in a compartment four bunks stacked high maybe 100 to a compartment. The first couple of days wasn't too bad, but when one got sick it started quite a few trying to bring up their last meal, and the odor of sickness was all over the place.

My being in charge of a galley crew took me away from the compartment till late evenings. By working I had three meals a day and then at noon meal (crew only) was the best meal. Sometimes hot bread, ice cream, steak and such. The work was constant and it was hot in the galley and the

17

crew did the usual bitching nothing that wasn't expected. At chow time it was a long line, starting at 7 A.M. to 9 A.M. for breakfast. Dinner started at 5 P.M. ended around 7 P.M. Generally we took an hour to clean up afterwards. My crew had a break during the day and was able to go on deck also at night.

Many card games were played; you name the game they played the same. While we were working the troops did exercises or field striped the rifle, all in keeping busy and the care of the rifle. I volunteered and since I was a staff sgt. I was given a crew to wash pots and trays. Volunteering paid off for me, it kept me busy and I didn't have time to worry about the ships rolling. Many of the fellows were sea sick and the compartment smelled like it. Showers aboard ship were sea water. The chow was pretty good. We were ten days aboard ship (Liberty Ship) time was heavy on our hands there was schedules for deck time. No smoking on deck at night. Movies and V.D. films were shown so the troops were purposely shown some bad cases of VD to make us learn the women. Some it never fazed us in any large group of people, we had all kinds of 'Hounds'.

Africa—

Then the landing in Africa. It was all strange. After debarking we were taken to a staging area outside of town. From there we boarded a train that took us across the mountains and northern part of the desert, all in cattle cars. The British prepared hot meals, lamb stew with lots of grease. Ugh. During the trip we had exchanges with the native Arabs. They would try to buy anything. If that didn't work they tried to steal it. It was a tiresome trip, but being in a new country and a different culture the trip went fast.

Arriving in Morocco, we were set up away outside of town. The one thing that stood out and well remembered was when rumor came around that there were some girls in the mountains. A couple of us climbed the hill to see what's it was all about. Well...I've heard about some women could take on an army, but that was the first time that I actually saw it. Standing on top of the hill looking down we saw four lines of soldiers, and at the bottom I suppose there was four or more girls. Each line must have been one hundred soldiers lined up.

Life on the desert was quite different. The heat at midday was over 90 degrees and dry. Movement in the day was very slow. But at all times you had to watch your clothes and equipment. The Arabs were always alert to anything that wasn't nailed down. There were times that the tent was cut and anything or everything was gone. With all the heat gone after sundown, you started putting on clothes. After going to sleep you wake up to put on anything and everything because it was cold. We learned to sleep in heavy clothes after the first night. I remember one trip to town, after looking around we started down the Red Light District. Women calling you from the windows and doors in all stages of dress. I still had the picture of the film I saw on board ship in mind and stayed away.

During this time Colonel Queen was sent back to the states and Col. Ferguson took command (Gentleman Ferguson). We were then told we were going to Italy, to guard the Airfields in the 15th Airforce. We boarded the British Ships and sailed to Italy. Aboard Ship we had plenty of tea and bread and mutton real greasy. One reason I don't like Mutton today.

Chapter VI

Italy

.

We stayed outside of Naples until we were assigned to Chernoglia, where the 15th Airforce had a bomb group.

We set up in an area close to the airfield. I was acting 1 Sgt. of the detachment of company I. I choose Pvt. Martin as a tent mate. He was an ex CCC camper. He helped put up the floor using bomb casing lumber, and using gasoline drums and copper tubing to heat up the tents. Also made a desk and a lock closet in the desk for the PX supplies. I was getting good so I made a lounge chair all out of the ammo casing.

One evening after a rough day on the Airfield were we was guarding planes, I returned to the tent and found the desk broken in to and a note was on the desk. The note said "I couldn't hold out any longer, will pay you back on pay day... I knew that Martin was a heavy drinker, but he had a hell of a lot more experience from the old CCC Camps. That's why when he first came in to the tent I told him if he stayed sober for a month I'd see he'd get his PFC Private first class stripe and each month another stripe. Martin did make corporal. Even though he showed us how to make an oil heating stove out of oil cans and tubing, put down a wood floor, built tables, chairs, outhouse, etc. But when he borrowed the PX money I had in the desk with other PX supplies that was the end of Martins NCO rank. We didn't see Martin for about a week.

We got a call from the French soldiers which were in the area that one of our men was drunk and disorderly and to come and get him. Martin had wound up with the French outfit and was trying to barter cigarettes for wine. Since we knew the French issued wine in 5 gallon cans, Martin must has tried to drink the 5 gallons. Needless to say Martin remained a private the rest of his army career.

One of our Staff Sgts. who was in the detachment received a letter from his wife, telling him not to pay more than five dollars for it because that's all she's getting for hers. We knew that they were separated, but still that's a hellava thing to be writing to a soldier over seas.

We had been here several months when someone drove a 6x6 truck (we had no vehicle that size) into camp with about eight or ten girls. It was after dark when they arrived. About midnight it got a little out of hand, and I had to send them on there way. One afternoon the 99th pursuit squadron flew over and landed. About an hour later they arrived at our camp stating that there was no "Colored" mess for the pilots and was directed to our area. You can imagine how bitter they felt. Here they were up in the air guarding their planes from the "Jerrys" from all reports it seems they preferred the 99th for over all coverage. Yet now on the ground it's a different atmosphere. When the 99th did leave they took off and came over the area with their salute, the barrel roll. It almost blew over our tents.

One day the bombers were returning from a bomb run, and the planes were landing, when we received a call to go to a plane which had crashed landed in a field several miles away. We were to go and secure the area until Airforce personnel arrived. When we got there no one was alive and body parts were all over the place. We secured the area until the medical units and authorized personnel arrived. After the bodies were removed and other military items removed, there were remaining some parachutes that were damaged and of no use. We took them. I took one and made sheets for my bunk. Cut them up to size and a little talcum powder and you had a beautiful wet dream. The sheets didn't last too long they kept getting messed up.

One period there in Charannola we had to do military police duty. I got to be known and was invited to a home which was having a family party. The "Old Man" brought out some wine from the basement, sparkling burgundy. I was drinking it like it was fruit punch. After a while I started feeling it. I got some of their black bread and one of the young children and sat down and had the kid on my knees playing with him until my head began to clear up again. About half hour later I got up and joined the party again doing a dance something like the square dance. The "Old Man" (head of the house) called me over and said I got zig zag (drunk) I laughed and said "poker poker, just a little." After that I had no problem with having my clothes cleaned since he was the town's cleaner. He liked the fact that I could control my drinking. We were friends until we were sent to the front.

One day our company officer Lt. Goode, told me to go to the South African Unit to coordinate guard duty between the two units. It was an order from the Air Field Headquarters. Well when I arrived there at the South Africans HQ. tent, I went in and stood there waiting to be acknowledged while the first Sgt. was looking busy at his desk. After a while he said something about my saluting him. Well I was a little pissed off because he kept me standing there. I told him off and told him when he's ready to do business he could come to my tent. I left there and called the post commander and told him the story. He apologized and said he would correct the situation. The next day the South African Sgt. was there to do business, at my tent....

We were relieved, and regrouped with the rest of the company. In Foggia we learned that we were going to the front and joined the 92nd Division. We entrucked and traveled north. Then by foot through bombed out towns, you could almost choke to death because of the odor of decay. On we went until we got to a holding area. When we left Charannola, we were told we were going to be attached to the 92nd Division as special troops of the 5th Army. Arriving at the assigned area, General Armond "greeted us." He spoke of the Negro Newspapers sent us over here, he didn't ask for us but since we are here we will fight.

We were supposed to get some training, but part of the Regt. was sent into activities on the front. Later we were given a position in the mountain. One side of the valley was the Germans. On a bright day we could see them walking about, the distance was too great for our rifles. There was a forward observation post which had to be manned that was closer to the enemy and down in the valley. My duties were the communication, I had to maintain wire from the observation post to command post also the rest of the company, and also maintain the wire, telephone, radio, and the company runners. Some times the Germans would tap the wire lines or cut them. The phones were not dependable. Most contact was with our radio a SCR 300. We later leaned that the Germans would tune in on the wave length and zero in with their guns 88's or mortar shells. We soon learned to keep our communications short and move the radio so it wouldn't be at one place too long. One night while we were in our "quarters" the ground floor of a hotel that was closed, we left the radio on and the 88 shells started coming in. Many patrols were sent out. I went on one with orders to check the town up ahead and the route to town. Also bring in any prisoners we could, but we were to avoid fighting if we could. We checked the town and found it empty, but we spotted several machine gun placements, and returned without any prisoners or any contact with the enemy. While we were up on the mountain, there was a steady stream of refugees and prisoners. We would escort them back to HQ. Sometimes there were blondes that could be Germans, we took special precautions with them. The trouble of going back to HQ. was it was all up hill coming back, and usually you carried ammo on your back. Sometimes HQ sent mules up with the ammo and food. If I remember right we were up on the line for about 50 days. A couple of times we heard that the Germans were getting ready to attack. Nothing came of it. One day we were ordered to make sure we had our dog tags on because the Durkers of India were coming through on a patrol We heard about the Durka's. Tales were they would infiltrate the enemy line and catch them sleeping, cut their heads off, and some in cases put the head on a live one. Cut their ears off, because one time they were paid for ears. They stopped paying for ears. Officials must have felt some friendly troops were missing ears. In any case we didn't see them come through our lines. A couple of days later we were relieved. They were getting ready for a push (attack). We went back to a center where they had portable showers and a change of clothes. You stripped at the entrance, then into the shower and on the other side you got a complete change of clothes. We were then sent back to the rest area in Florence.

Our next assignment was in the coastal area pushing up the coast. I had just returned from the hospital recovering from a bad cold. I was assigned to a machine gun placement, while the rest of the company pushed up along the coast. The 10th Mountain Rangers on the right flank to protect us from the Germans in the mountain area. The 10th was to push first to keep the mountains clear so the shells would not hinder our push up the coast. We heard that the MP's had to come up to keep the 10th from retreating. All this time we were getting the hell beat out of us from the shelling off the mountains on our right. I remember going up for something and just off the canal were several tanks which were out of action. The tank commander, a captain, was behind the tank asking for cover so he could get his men back. I had choice words for him. I don't remember, but I left him there. Just before the attack the engineers were trying to put a bridge across the canal so the tanks and other vehicles could cross. They were having a hard time. The shells from the mountains keep knocking out the platoon bridges they were putting up.

During the day of the push (attack), I received orders to take some men and go to the canal and set up the machine guns. Orders were confusing but I sent some men up in event there was a break through and they might need cover to return.

December 1944, I was the NCO in charge of a machine gun placement. We had several stationary positions setup for "scheduled" firing. We had orders for a back up in event the Germans tried to break through. This particular night I was just sitting around when a runner from the company headquarters came up and said I was ordered back to the company HQ. Well I was a little disturbed and at the same time glad I was going back with the whole company. That was until I got to the company area. Arriving at the company area I found everybody loading up with hand grenades and extra rounds of ammo, and stripping down to just the necessary equipment for a raid. I reported to Captain Overall who told me I was leading the company across the Chinqualie Canal. He showed me on the map where we were going and told me we were going on a raid for prisoners. My duties were to find a crossing on the canal for the company of some one hundred fifty men. Well my heart started beating loud enough for everybody to hear. I went out and got my equipment and left all my personal stuff like everybody else with the supply Sgt. About that time we were beginning to line up for departure. As we started out to the line of departure, with the night darkness surrounding us, we waited for the time to start our raid. When I was given order to pull out, I started saying my prayers, knowing I am the first to cross into enemy territory and being exposed searching for good cover and a place to cross the canal. Thinking of my family back home where I wished I was right then. Well I swallowed a couple of times and started across the canal. I was lucky my path took me across the first time finding a suitable crossing for the company to follow. After the company got on the other side, the Capt. said we go up the beach for about 1,000 yards and turn in. But, when we got to that point it was high ground, and the Capt. said to go further down the beach so we could cross at a low point. When we got to a suitable spot, he told me to scout the area. First I went across the road and found a house with a walled in area and he brought the raiding party across. Then I was told to scout the road for fifty feet or so. I had taken two men with me going down the road, and not more than twenty feet or so from the company when all hell broke loose. A machine gun opened up at us, on my side of the road. The bullets seemed to go all around me. My cartridge belt seemed to sparkle and I felt a tug on my sleeve and pants. Then I dropped to the ground, trying to pin point where the gun was. I heard somebody running in the direction of the shooting. I waited a few more minutes and turned around and went back to the group. Now, all that stuff in the movies about being shot, I didn't know I was shot until someone mentioned it, that I had a hole in my pants.

I couldn't see where it came out, but it went in on the right side of my hip. Somebody gave me some water and a pill. The Capt. told me to get a couple of men and go back the way we came. Incidentally, the two men with me got back. As I started back to the end of the company I asked for a couple of men to return with me. Damn, it looked like half of the third platoon wanted to go back with me. The Platoon Sgt picked out a couple and I started back. By the time I got to the beach and headed back there were four or five men with me. Well I told them to stay at the water's edge which was ground level and we might avoid some of the bullets shot over our head. Some of the group felt better swimming and was out in water deep enough for them to swim beyond the breakers. Those who were out in the ocean swimming back never made it. That was where the bullets seemed to be hitting, going over the heads of those who were with me. Well we crawled damn near the whole two or three thousands yards. I went beyond the "front" lines because I didn't want anybody who might be trigger happy to think we were the enemy. Well at one point I said we have to go inland across the beach. We crossed the beach and came to a wall and troops were up on top. After the challenge we were allowed to come up on street level. They told us that we came through a mine field. Well it was no need worrying now that we came through it, and I was beginning to hurt. My knees were all raw from the sand and crawling, plus my butt was starting to sting. I was put on a jeep and sent back to the Aid Station. The others I guess were sent back to the company area. After cleaning the wound and dressing it, I was put on a holding area. About this time some of the wounded patrol starting coming in. That's when I learned Capt. Overall didn't make it, nor Sgt. Mahaley. The 2nd Platoon I was told got captured. Other names were being called off were either missing, wounded or dead. I was getting sleepy and must have dozed off. I don't remember the trip to Pisa General Hospital.

My stay in Pisa at the hospital was interesting. A day after arriving in the hospital the head ward nurse (she was from the midwest) was making her rounds. She stopped at my bed and asked how I was doing. After looking at me, she noticed sand was still in my hair and I guess I was a sight since I'd not been washed up since entering the field or General Hospital. She asked me if anybody attempted to wash me, I said no. Muttering something she left. Shortly after she left one of the floor nurses came with a pan of water and towel etc. and proceeded to clean me up. She was the same nurse that showed me the bed the day before. Later the head nurse returned to see how I was doing. We struck up a conversation about the lackadaisical manner some of the nurses had. But after that I had no more trouble. A couple of days later the doctor said I could start eating in the mess hall since my wound seemed to recovering well. After that I started visiting around the ward, playing cards and other games. One day we were playing whist when one of the players got very excited about the hand he had. Over zealously started to play, forgetting he only had one hand. He went to grab the card with his right hand but it was only a nub, cut off at the wrist. The other players realizing what had happened got quiet and all of us were a little depressed. Needless to say the game was over.

After about ten days I was shipped to a "Repo Depo" Company for reassignment. There must have been about 100 to 150 soldiers from all over. I was called to the office, and told since I was the senior Non Commissioned Officer I was to act as the 1st Sgt. and call the roll at all formations. Being from an all black outfit I was used to names like the Jones, Smith, Williams etc., but this list was like reading the United Nations roll call. I looked around, up and down the line until I found a studious Jewish soldier, called him up and told him he was the company clerk, and give him the rooster to call.

Later I was asked if I wanted to go back to my outfit or be reassigned. I was told I could go back to my outfit but on limited assignment so I headed back up to the front. On arriving at the outfit, I was brought up to date, who was shot, wounded, captured, missing etc.

While I was gone, our company clerk was performing the duties of the first Sgt. when there was a surprise inspection and review. The general wanted to know why a corporal was acting 1st Sgt. The general stated if he's acting make him. So the Company Clerk Redding was made 1st Sgt. Since I was on limited duty, I was returned to my Machine Gun Placement.

First Sgt. Redding called me from the machine gun emplacement to help him with the attack plans of the company. There was a push on. The 101 Mountain Battalion was to secure the mountains on the right and Company I to go up the coast road crossing the Chinqulale Canal. Redding had orders to go with the company, in charge of company headquarters. I was ordered to remain in the company area with the cooks and other men who were left behind. The company left early in the morning. We back in the company area got bits and pieces of what was happening. Seems that the 101st Mountain Company didn't secure the right flank causing heavy fire power from the mountains right down on the costal area and the company. Much confusion during the day such as receiving orders to take the machine guns up to the Chinquale Canal and set up to fire on anything that come across the canal. Also to round up all able bodied men to reinforce the line. Towards night fall stragglers began to return to the company. We were trying to find out what was happening, what happened to the rest of the company, just anything we could get. Most couldn't tell much only those they saw got killed. Seems it was hot and heavy on the line. Some 150 to 200 men who went up that morning only about thirty returned. Battalion HQ called and told me to reform the company, that 130 replacements were on the way. When the company moved out and left me in charge of the cooks and misfits who didn't or couldn't go on the raid. That was one of my longest nights. Just sitting around drinking coffee and waiting for news, any news about the raid. Around midnight stragglers started returning. They looked bad. Since I went to the hospital after the last raid I had no idea of the worry or turmoil that went with waiting the return of the company. You started asking about your friends, officers, anything to get an idea of what the situation was. Well the casualties were high again. We lost Redding and about 2/3's of the men. Around 2 A.M. I received orders from Bn HQ to reform the company. Also was told there was replacement coming in the morning over 100 men. We were sent back to the staging area to reform and retrain.

We were then sent back to an area to reform. Lt. M. Walker was sent to the company to take over as company commander. The company was formed and I as the 1st Sgt turned the company over to Lt. Walker. He took the report and company and stated he didn't want me as his first Sgt., and to step down and he'll appoint someone. I took my post wondering what was happening. The next morning as per usual I formed the company, took the report, and turned to the duty officer, who happen to be Lt. Walker. He again informed me that I was to step down. Well I couldn't wait until after formation to go to headquarters to see the colonel. When I arrived at headquarters and informed the Sgt. Major of the problem and asked to see the colonel I was sent right in. I informed the colonel that I was under the impression that he was the only one who made 1st Sgts. and broke 1st Sgts. After a few questions he informed me that he would look into it.

I returned to the company area. That evening at the last formation retreat, Lt. Walker received a message from headquarters to report at once. Lt. Walker never returned to Company I. but was reassigned to Headquarters. Lt. Goode became acting Company Commander until we received a new Company Commander.

While in the staging area reforming the company several things happened to me. One was my wallet was returned. After I went to the hospital all my possessions were either stolen or lost. One night while sitting in my tent someone threw my wallet in the tent. Picking it up realizing it was mine, I went to the tent entrance to see if I could find the one who threw it in. No such luck. The wallet had no money nor pictures. My wife and daughter's pictures were in the wallet. I swore if I found someone showing my wife's picture around he wouldn't be able to do it again.

Another evening Sgt. McDowell came in with a pint of American whiskey, something which is rare. He wanted to share it with me and he had been drinking. Well I didn't want anything that night and told him so, but since we had done quite a bit of drinking together, he insisted on my having some and kept at it until I got angry and grabbed the bottle and threw it out of the tent and it broke. Well you can imagine Mac's attitude and a few choice words. He left. Other than in the line of duty Mac didn't speak to me again.

We were given leave to go to the rest area near Florence. First we stopped over at one of those moving supply centers where we were able to take a shower and get clean clothes then off to the big city. After looking at some of the sights we checked out the Red Cross for a little recreation. Oh, and it was a very little recreation for us the black soldier. Coming back from the front with no money we felt the Red Cross would give us cigarettes and ice cream and donuts. But to our surprise again cigarettes were five cents and donut and coffee fifteen cents. All was not lost since the Salvation Army was down the street and the donuts and coffee plus cigarettes were free. (That incident caused a little trouble at home when I returned. My daughter had asked me for ten cents for the Red Cross, because they were having a drive on. Well my feelings of the Red Cross came out when I denied my daughter ten cents. My wife I believe gave her the money to take to school because all the other kids were giving and the school she was attending was majority white then. Another reason why I had a bad feeling for the Red Cross was when in Chernagila, Italy, guarding planes of the 15th Air Force a request for blood went out to all outfits. We marched to the blood center as a unit and it was noted that our blood was separated from the other blood that was being drawn. There was a time when I thought the Red Cross made a mistake and came up to the staging area and gave us coffee and donuts.

After the cease fire we were sent to a little town on highway 67. For the life of me I could not tell you what we were doing there. We occupied several buildings, one for company HQ, one for our new Capt. Percy Daniels, had taken over a private house for himself. Each platoon had a building.

I took the top floor of another house. We had a motor pool and a truck loaded with gas. Shortly after we were settled in Capt. Daniel noticed that we were missing a lot of gasoline. He complained so much that I put two guards covering the motor pool, one at the front entrance and one on the back entrance. That still did not stop the missing gas. One night after hearing the Capt. complaining, I stayed up to watch what happened at the motor pool to see what was really happening. While waiting to see what happened I notice a driver go to Capt. Daniel's house, then to the motor pool, take the gas truck out and later return and go to the Captain's quarters after parking the truck. I didn't check to see what driver it was, but checked with the guard and found out he was given a note from the Capt. to release the truck. The next morning I was in the office doing the morning report, when the Capt. came in raising hell again about the gas shortage. After listening to him complain, I mentioned that all the gas was there except the gas he OK'd. There was silence in the room for a while. Then he said ok. We never had any more shortages.

Some time later after sitting on pillows I went to the hospital for hemorrhoids. The operation was simple so the doctor said. I had a spinal tap and could see and hear everything that was going on. The doctors were talking about their nights activities. I told them not to get excited about last night especially while they were cutting on my rear end. My first thought when I woke up was to sit up. Luckily a nurse was there and told me to remain with my head down, or I'll have a helluva hangover. Then the sis baths, soothing, but the first movement, oh-boy.

After ten days I was back with the outfit they were still on highway 67. Shortly after, we were reassigned to a railroad depot in the city of Modena. We were guarding the supplies and Italian prisoners. The prisoners were doing the work around the depot. We stayed there a short time then back to a staging area. At the staging area the 366th Infantry Regiment was deactivated, and became the 224 and 226 Combat engineers. I was assigned to the 224th Engineers.

Chapter VII

Returning to U.S.A.

During this transition period we trained and attempted to be come engineers. Shortly after, maybe several weeks when news filtered down that the soldiers with enough points (if I remember it was over 100 points) would be shipped home. We were given the options of either fly or by boat. I was one of about 100 who choose to go by plane, the fastest route.

About 100 of us, mostly the first three grades, were all shipped to the 92 Engrs, who were being shipped home. But we were put up for what we thought would be a short time. Talking with the 92nd Engrs we learned that their colonel imposed fines on his men for fraternizing with the Italian, especially the women. We later learned that all of the fines he imposed on his men he kept and never entered it on the service record. When we heard the news being circulated around the 366 men was to replace his men, we marched to his tent in total, and armed and loaded for bear. In unity we stated we were attached to this outfit for shipment home, not a replacement for that outfit. He stood before his tent with his .45 Colt and ordered us back, or he'd shoot. We informed him that he may shoot one or two, but he'd never see or hear the third shot. After a discussion to "save face," he indicated he would cut orders to ship us to Naples, repro depo staging area. The next day we had enough trucks to ship all of us out and each of us could have had a truck. After in Naples a while, we heard the same colonel in charge of the 92Engrs. used to fine his troops for talking or fraternizing with the Italian girls, or restrict them to the Regt. Area or other such punishment. We heard that the Criminal Investigation Div. (CID) had picked him up for "pocketing" the fines he had imposed on the troops and was relived of his command. I never heard the outcome, or had it verified that it was true.

While in Naples we were told we would be informed of date and time of shipping out, and it would be to Africa then to the states. Also we could buy coupons for the bar (two dollars per book) each ticket was ten cents for beer or whiskey. We bought a book each since we didn't know when we would be shipped out. We had a free day to look over Naples before we were posted to be shipped out.

We were finally flown to Africa and told that we would be at the airfield about three days then home.

We were close to the Mediterranean Theater Command Headquarters or closer to the airfield.

I noticed that there were a lot of troops from the Asian Command mostly black. We were assigned to tents and told to watch the bulletin board for our scheduled flight, which would not be over three days.

A few hours later a couple of soldiers who had been there for a month or so complained to me that the white soldiers were being shipped out but only a handful of the blacks were leaving. I asked why didn't he complain to the other 1st sgts. from the Asian Command. He told me that they won't talk up to the white officer. I told him I'd look into it no promises.

Next day I noticed that flight schedules did not include many names that I could recognized as being black.

The flight officer, a 1st lt (white) the only officer in the area, I complained to him. He told me he received the names from Med. Theater Command HQ and he just posted them. I asked permission to speak to the post commander and got an OK. The post commander said he was in charge of the post and had no authority over flights, which come from Med. Theater Command. I than requested permission to go to Command HQ. I took the bus the next day to MTC. Arriving at a tall building and not knowing a soul, I took a deep breath and entered. At the information desk I requested to speak to the commanding general. I was referred to a colonel who asked what business I had with the commanding general. I explained my situation at the airfield fully. I was told that I'd be able to get a better answer from the colonel in charge of flights. When I got to the "Flight Colonel" and explained the situation, he came back at me hard asking if I was trying to get home earlier. When I explained that some of the troops were there for a month or more, which meant that I would possibly be there for a month or more. We were told in Naples we would be here

31

only three days. He seemed to calm down and explained that Fla. airfield wasn't taking black soldiers so they have to be sent to NYC. I said all well and good all the white soldiers can go to Fla. and blacks to NYC. He came back and said there were a lot of white soldiers living in the north that's why he's sending them there. I was getting warm, and said that I'd call my father who lives in Washington (for all the good that would do) and see if he can help straighten this out. He started up and we were kicking it back and forth. Finally he said, he'll take another look at the schedules and for me to go back to camp.

When I got back to camp everybody wanted to know what happened. I explained and said we will have to wait and see. I was called to the flight office and was questioned by the flight officer who gave me permission that started me on the quest to get home. He praised me stating he wish he'd had a sgt. in his outfit that fought for his men like I did. That afternoon when the evening flights were placed on the bulletin board, it seemed like all the black soldiers were listed to leave that night and the next day. Leaving Africa I had three bottles of Hennessey Star cognac...Flying over the desert the plane dropped several hundred feet at one time, we were sitting in mid-air when we leveled off. I was leveling off a bottle of my cognac. A little later it happened again, then there were two bottles of cognac gone. Once we were past the desert we had clear sailing in to Bermuda where we landed and had lunch. Going through the chow line the girls looked good, and like we did in Italy we talked about the girls, until we came to the cashier who spoke the Queens English that sent us to the floor with red faces.

I was given the service records of the group going to Ft Hamilton NY. Arriving at the airfield we were told we had seven days to get to Ft. Dix for separation.

I arrived home, but the wife was working. The gang came over to welcome me home. The next day I got sick with a fever and temperature and had to call the hospital. The ambulance came but wouldn't take me since I was still in the service. Sent for the VA ambulance took me to the Bronx VA Hospital. I was in the Bronx Hospital for a week when they closed it and sent me to Staten Island Hospital. The records were sent on to Ft. Dix. After I recovered I was sent to Ft Dix. Fort Dix was now a center for separation. In the Mess Hall I heard a familiar voice, no other voice was like that of 1st Sgt C. Martin McNeal. Almost five years ago he and his outfit left which got me in the service. Now here again he left me and got home before me. I didn't complete my discharge until after midnight. 2 Oct 1945.

Chapter VIII

366th Infantry Veterans Association Activities

Couple of months later I was walking on 125 street in Harlem and met Col. Queen. He remembered me. We talked and he asked me if I was getting a pension.

I said no. He told me to come to his office and wrote the address. Later we met and he wrote up my disability pension. The 366th Infantry Veterans Assn. in New York was formed by Vander W. Mack and Jack Barnes, both were living in Brooklyn, in 1946. I was not aware of the forming of the Assn. One afternoon in 1956, while driving with my wife on Farmers Blvd in Queens, NY, I was hailed by Charles (Sonny) Avery, who I had not seen since the first raid in December 1944. We blocked traffic until one of us decided to move to the curb and continue to try to catch up on the past couple of years in a short time. Well, we exchanged addresses and telephone numbers. That was my start in getting back together with some of the 6's. My four years and 6 months with the 6's had instilled a comradeship that I still felt and was glad to seek other veterans. Later I had received a Sixes Review bulletin which was published by John Philip Waring. We struggled to maintain the Assn. through to 1972. A few of us tried to keep it up. Charles Avery, Charles Fisher Chaplain, Robert Smith, Charles Scott and myself, attended the Reunions in Washington, D.C., Philadelphia, Fort Devens, Mass.

During the time from 1956 to 72, we gave dances which we tried to get as many of the outfit together. We had a trip to Italy that Vander Mack put together and the 366 Chapter seemed to die out after that.

The following pages I have put together some of the news articles that were sent to me and other articles that have come into my possession.

The reunion of the 366th Infantry Regt. was its 42 anniversary in May 1983. The Veterans of the 6's from Boston, Washington, and with a little help from Avery and myself, held Memorial Services at Ft. Devens. Attending from NYC were Charles Avery, Charles Scott, Robert Smith, Chaplain Fisher and myself, along with our spouses. Well Friday night at dinner, checking to see who was there I knew, and renewing old friendships, when someone mentioned that Whittaker was here. Well I must have passed him several times, but when I was directed to where he was, I knew him right away. Yes he was a little older, as we all were. We greeted each other like lost brothers. Didn't know what to say first. I learned that Sgt. Lucky and 1st Sgt. Fortson lived in his area. Our wives met and talked as we were doing.

It was an enjoyable weekend. Pictures, handouts etc. Visited the old barrack area (now a hospital took the whole Regt'l area). We visited the surrounding area, including the Mirror Lake. Saturday was the parade and presentation of the flags. The presentation of the Silver Star to Lt. Fox's widow was performed by a General who originally started as a private and now a Major General James F. Hamlet. Sunday services at the old Regt'l site where a plaque of the 366th Infantry Regt once stood, to commemorate our being stationed there.